# ESSENTIAL SPORTS

# hockey

ESSENTIAL SPORTS – HOCKEY
was produced by

**David West ☩ Children's Books**
7 Princeton Court
55 Felsham Road
London SW15 1AZ

*First published in Great Britain by* Heinemann Library. Heinemann Library is an imprint of **Pearson Education Limited,** a company incorporated in England and Wales having its registered office at Edinburgh Gate, Harlow, Essex CM20 2JE - Registered company number: 00872828

*Designed by*: Rob Shone
*Edited by*: James Pickering
*Picture Research by*: Carlotta Cooper
*Printed in* China

ISBN 978 0 431173 88 7 (hardback)
12 11 10 09 08
10 9 8 7 6 5 4 3 2 1
ISBN 978 0 431173 95 5 (paperback)
12 11 10 09 08
10 9 8 7 6 5 4 3 2 1

British Library Cataloguing in Publication Data

Smith, Andy
Hockey. - (Essential Sports)
1. Field Hockey - Juvenile literature
I. Title
796.3'55

A full catalogue record for this book is available from the British Library.

**Acknowledgements:**
We would like to thank the following for permission to reproduce photographs:

Pages 3, 4-5m, 14t, 22t (Scott Barbour), 5, 8tr & br, 26r, 28r (Simon Bruty), 7b, 10 both, 10-11, 14m, 15b, 17m, 18 both, 19l, 20 all, 24t, 25l, 30 (Stanley Chou), 11, 29t (Mike Powell), 12, 22b, 28l (Alex Livesey), 12-13, 16t, 24b (Jack Atley), 17t, 19r, 23b, 25r (Adam Pretty), 21 (Nick Laham), 23t (Al Bello), 26l (Ezra Shaw), 26-27 (Elsa Hasch), 29b (Mike Hewitt), 4-5t, 6 both, 6-7, 7m, 8tl, 15m, 16b, 27 - Getty Images. 8ml & m - Wisden advertisement is reproduced by kind permission of John Wisden & Co. Ltd. 8bl, 9 all - DITA International B.V. (Netherlands) / DITA Field Hockey, LLC (USA).
*Abbreviations: t-top, m-middle, b-bottom, r-right, l-left, c-centre.*

Cover photograph reproduced with permission of Getty Images.

Every effort has been made to contact copyright holders of material reproduced in this book. Any omissions will be rectified in subsequent printings if notice is given to the publishers.

**Disclaimer:**
All the Internet addresses (URLs) given in this book were valid at the time of going to press. However, due to the dynamic nature of the Internet, some addresses may have changed, or sites may have changed or ceased to exist since publication. While the author and Publishers regret any inconvenience this may cause readers, no responsibility for any such changes can be accepted by either the author or the Publishers.

*An explanation of difficult words can be found in the glossary on page 31.*

# ESSENTIAL SPORTS
# hockey

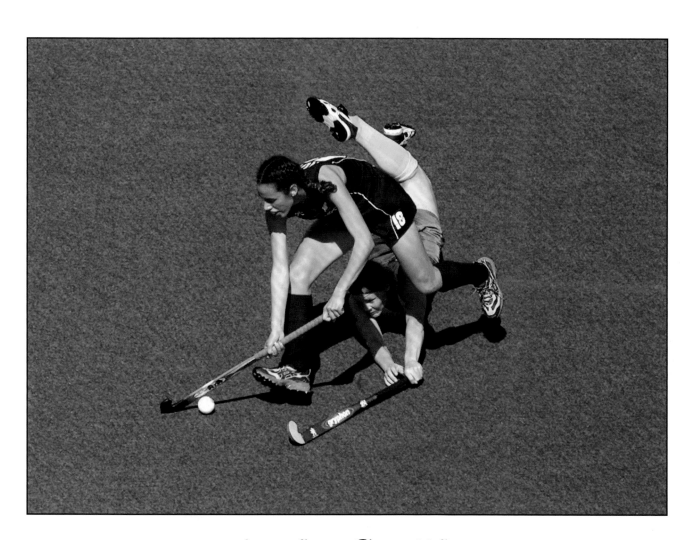

## Andy Smith

Heinemann
LIBRARY

# Contents

*Nadine Ernsting Krienke – Germany's most capped player – during their successful gold medal campaign at the 2004 Olympics in Athens.*

*The hockey centre in the Helliniko Olympic Complex, venue for the 2004 Olympic finals in Athens.*

*Hockey sticks are always in demand in India.*

# Introduction

Hockey is derived from a number of ancient stick and ball games, although it was not known as hockey until the late 18th century. In its modern form, it is reckoned to be the fastest team game in the world, and it has become even quicker since the 1980s with the widespread use of artificial pitches. The stronghold of the game is in India and Pakistan, though it is widely played in Australia (the current men's Olympic champions), Germany (women's Olympic champions in Athens) and in Great Britain, where England Hockey alone has over a thousand affiliated clubs. The inaugural 2007 Great Britain Super League men's and women's titles were both won by Wessex Leopards against teams from Scotland, Wales and the rest of England.

# History of the game

**H**ow did hockey begin? Probably when one of our ancestors picked up a stick and hit a stone down a track.

### WILD BEGINNINGS

Drawings on ancient tombs in the Nile Valley depict two men holding sticks with curved ends, with a ball in between them. As the tombs were built around 2,000 BC, it is assumed that the game has been around for about 4,000 years. Therefore hockey is the forerunner of all sports played with an implement, such as cricket, golf and polo. Hockey has similarities with the Irish sport of hurling, which dates back to 1,300 BC. The Romans played a game called paganica, in which a ball, filled with feathers, was propelled with a club.

*Shinty evolved in Scotland from a game said to have been played by Celtic legends. Apparently, King Alexander of Scotland was a good player in the 12th century.*

*By the 1920s, hockey was regarded all around the world to be a women's game.*

### THE FORMATIVE YEARS

Hockey was played in English public schools in Victorian times, while the first club, Blackheath in south east London, was formed around 1861. It was a rough game, played in a massive area of 247 metres by 64. A national association was set up in 1886, and the first international, Wales against Ireland, was played in 1895. Early forms of hockey were considered too barbaric for women to play, but the first women's club, Moseley Ladies in west London, was founded in 1887.

*In the 20th century, hockey became a favourite sport for girls at school.*

## COMPETITION

Olympic hockey was first played in 1908 in London, when Britain won gold, but the sport was not included in 1924, as it did not have an international ruling body. The International Federation was formed immediately, though the British Hockey Association did not join until 1970. Until recently, hockey was one of the few remaining amateur sports. Today, coaches and players may be paid.

## A GAME OF TWO HALVES ...

British women's hockey remained separate from the men's association until 1997, over 100 years after the first women's club was formed. Progress of the women's game was hampered by the idea that the game should not be played for prizes or rewards – an attitude which persisted until the 1960s – and concerns about the clothing worn on the field.

*The Netherlands won the 2007 World Cup by beating Australia 3-1.*

*At the 1952 Olympics, the Netherlands and West Germany used old-fashioned English sticks.*

## INDIAN STICKS

India's first hockey clubs were started in the 1880s. As a measure of how quickly the game rose in popularity there, India won Olympic gold for the first time in 1928, and went on to win at the next five Olympic Games! In the 1950s, Indian hockey stick makers introduced a stick with a short toe which gave better control. It soon came into general use, replacing the longer and heavier English stick.

# Kit

Like most sports, hockey has developed over the years, not least in the quality of the kit available.

*Hockey kit in the 1920s borrowed from other sports – especially cricket and soccer.*

## KIT DEVELOPMENT

Little is known about the kit used in early forms of hockey until 1867, when boys at Tonbridge School in Kent are said to have made their own sticks from branches, cut from nearby woods and bent into shape. Early women players had to wear skirts that reached within 25 mm of the ground, and straw hats!

*The Indian national team in their dressing room cluttered with kit*

*A 1930s advert for Wisden hockey kit*

*The outdoor stick weighs up to 800 g.*

*Indoor stick*

*Goalkeeper's stick*

## STICKS

Most woods have been used to make hockey sticks – even oak in the early days. Holly and maple were tried until the 1920s when the standard stick was ash with a cane handle. By the 1950s, Indian stick manufacturers were using mulberry, which can be easily shaped. Today, some sticks have a polyurethane plastic finish. Others are stiffened with fibreglass.

*Hockey sticks being made in India, 1996.*

## THE BALL

Different balls are used on different surfaces. Leather balls are best on grass, while dimpled plastic balls are used on artificial turf. In senior games the ball weighs about 155 g, and 100 g in youngsters' hockey.

*Balls used in indoor hockey are usually white or yellow.*

## TECH TIPS – PLAYER PROTECTION

*As hockey is such a fast game, played with a hard ball, every player must be adequately protected from injury. Gum shields and shin guards are essential. Shin guards can vary from pads covering the lower shin, to prosthetic guards covering the ankle and the whole shin bone.*

*The development of protective equipment has been extensive in the modern game.*

## BOOTS

You should choose boots that feel the most comfortable, with plenty of support for the foot and heel. Use long studs in wet conditions, short studs where it's firmer. On artificial turf, wear pimpled soles. For comfort, some players choose boots that are half a size too big and wear an extra pair of socks.

*Today, hockey boots are smart, durable and comfortable.*

## GOALKEEPER'S KIT

This specialized position requires special kit. Wearing a helmet takes some getting used to, and it is no use having one that does not fit properly and obscures your view in any direction. Right and left gloves differ. The right, or the stick holding hand, has padding on the outside, while the left is padded on the inside to prevent bruising when stopping shots with the hand.

*Being in the most exposed position, the goalkeeper needs special equipment.*

HELMET

THROAT GUARD

CHEST AND ARM GUARD

STICK GLOVE

LEFT GLOVE

HIP AND THIGH GUARD

GROIN PROTECTOR

SHIN GUARD

KICKING BOOTS

# Rules of the game

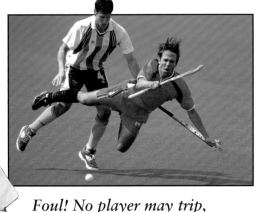

*Foul! No player may trip, push, strike or handle another player.*

F or a game in which the ball frequently moves at speeds up to 160 km/h – it's no surprise that two umpires are needed.

### GAME AIMS

Simply, the main aim of the game is to score more goals than the opposition, and so win the match. The goals are twelve feet wide and seven feet high. These are smaller than football goals, but nobody is allowed to shoot from outside a 16-yard area. So, you often see a defensive line-up with all the players from one team lined up in a wall, blocking the route to goal.

*Umpires carry three cards – green is a warning, yellow sends offenders off the field for at least five minutes, red expels them from the rest of the game.*

*A penalty stroke is a one against one shot from the penalty stroke line, awarded when a foul prevents a likely goal. The goalie must remain behind the goal line until the ball is hit.*

## RULES

The ball may only be hit with the flat side of the stick and outfield players may not use their feet to control the ball. Generally the ball may not be hit in the air but, if controlled, can be 'scooped' or 'lifted' to pass or shoot as long as it is not dangerous for another player. Obstruction is also foul play, whether by player or stick against an opponent or by blocking a player making an attempt to reach the ball (third party obstruction). These days there is no offside rule in hockey.

## OFFICIALS

The umpires, in conjunction with a timekeeper, keep control of the game. The umpires take one half of the pitch each, operating from opposite sidelines. In the early days, an umpire could only give a decision after an appeal had been made by one of the sides. In the early 1900s that changed, so that the umpires had complete charge.

## TECH TIPS – UMPIRES' AREAS OF RESPONSIBILITY

*Pitch measurements were drawn up when imperial units (inches, feet and yards) were used instead of metric units. One yard equals 0.914 metres. Standing on opposite sidelines, umpires are responsible for the whole area inside one 25-yard line and for half the area between the two 25-yard lines. Here, umpires deal with fouls coming towards them. The diagram below shows how this works.*

*Good positioning by the umpire as Australia score against Spain.*

# Pitch and positions

Legend has it that Native American tribes played a form of hockey lasting several hours, with the goals kilometres apart and about 1,000 players on each side. Times have changed!

*Games on synthetic pitches are rarely called off, even in heavy rain.*

## THE PITCH

Top class games are played on full-sized pitches. The field should be 100 yards long by 60 yards wide. This gives internationals and top class players room to move, and pass accurately and quickly. Less experienced players are better suited to a smaller pitch, perhaps 60 yards long and 45 yards wide. Synthetic surfaces are rapidly taking over from natural grass.

## MARKINGS

These are 3 inches wide. The centre line divides the pitch into two halves. The sidelines and backlines indicate when the ball is out of play. A penalty corner can be awarded for a foul within the 25-yard lines. Goals may be scored within the shooting circles, and penalties must be taken from the penalty spot.

*The Warsteiner Park in Mönchengladbach was the setting for the 2006 men's World Cup Final.*

**SIDE LINE**

**SHOOTING CIRCLE**
*The goalkeeper cannot kick the ball outside the shooting circle. The ball cannot be lofted deliberately into this area from a distance away.*

100 yds (92.5 m)

**BACK LINE**

5 yds (4.5 m)

7 yds (6.5 m)

**PENALTY SPOT**

10 yds (9 m)

16 yds (14.5 m)

60 yds (55.5 m)

**10-YARD MARK**

*A full-sized pitch marked out for a game.*

## TECH TIPS – ZONES

*The most important task when attacking is to keep possession of the ball. When defending, your aim is to regain the ball. Each side should use every area, or zone, of the field to gain an advantage over the opposition, whether they are attacking or defending (right).*

If the attacking side knocks the ball over the back line, the defence restarts the game with a 16-yard hit-out.

If the defending side accidentally knocks the ball over the back line, the attacking side restarts the game with a hit or push from the 5-yard mark.

A ball deliberately knocked over the back line by the defending side gives the attacking side a penalty corner from the 10-yard mark.

When the ball goes over the side line, the game is restarted with a push or hit. The side touching the ball last gives away possession.

CENTRE LINE

25-YARD LINE
All players except the goalkeeper and penalty taker must be beyond this line during penalty strokes. Penalties are awarded for fouls committed inside the shooting circle.

16-YARD MARK

25 yds (23 m)

16 yds (14.5 m)

5-YARD MARK

5 yds (4.5 m)

3 in (7.5 cm)
2 in (5 cm)

7 feet (2.1 m)

18 in (46 cm)

GOAL LINE

4 yds (3.7 m)

### SURFACES

Hockey was almost always played on natural grass until about 25 years ago – it was called 'field hockey' in the USA to separate it from 'ice hockey'. The game is much faster on synthetic surfaces, and they require much less attention than grass fields. The last major tournament on grass was the 1982 World Cup.

## TECH TIPS – THE PLAYERS

*The usual formation, especially in schools, is the 1-2-3-5 line-up (below). Sometimes, the inside forwards are withdrawn towards midfield, making a 1-2-3-2-3 formation.*

Goalkeeper

Right back          Left back

Right half     Centre half     Left half

Right wing   Inside right   Centre forward   Inside left   Left wing

13

# Goalkeeping

*Korean goalkeeper Ko Dong Sik charges out to block a shot.*

Artificial pitches and the development of protective equipment have radically changed goalkeeping. But the goalkeeper's essential skills never change – confidence and bravery.

## HANDLING THE BALL

Peter Mills, the England goalkeeper in the 1970s, was the first to stop high balls with his left hand. This is more difficult than it sounds, because it is against the rules to hold the ball or propel it forwards. Keepers can deflect the ball wide of the goal, or if the shot is coming straight at them, use the flat of the hand to drop the ball downwards but not forwards. Modern gloves make this a less painful exercise than in Mills's day.

## POSITIONING

In general, the goalkeeper stands between the ball and the centre of the goal to narrow the angle available to the attacker. As the player moves into the circle, the keeper advances a stride or two off the line. If the ball is passed, the keeper must move to a new position to cover the new angle of attack.

*Move off the line to confront the attacker and narrow the angle.*

## TECH TIPS – ANGLES

*A goalkeeper should be adjusting position at all times according to the whereabouts of the ball. When facing a lone attacker, the keeper should force the attacker to go to the keeper's open or stronger side.*

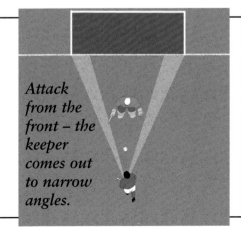

*Attack from the front – the keeper comes out to narrow angles.*

*Attack from the side – keeper stays back and guards goalpost, leaving narrow shooting angle on one side.*

## SKILL DRILL – SHOT STOPPING

This is an exercise that improves skills and sharpens up reactions. The keeper starts on the knees, and the feeder hits the ball to either side. The keeper dives to save, then immediately gets back on to the knees to stop the next shot.

*Practise diving with your legs together to form a solid barrier.*

*Practise with a team mate using light training balls or tennis balls.*

*Try the same routine from a squatting, then a standing position. Other players can be used to hit rebounds.*

## USING THE STICK

It is not always possible to use the pads or the left glove to save every shot. The goalkeeper should be prepared to use the stick for shots that are out of normal reach. The keeper should be balanced, weight slightly forwards, eyes on the ball. React to the ball and aim to use the left hand. But if this is impossible, when the ball is high and wide of the keeper, use the length of the right arm and the stick to stop the shot.

*Eyes on the ball, weight forwards, use the pads to block the shot.*

*When the ball is out of reach of the left hand, use the stick.*

## KICKING

A goalkeeper should use his pads to stop low, straight shots. Stay poised, leaning forwards so your weight will provide momentum, and keep your eyes on the ball. As the shot comes in, thrust the pad forwards with your head over the knee, and block it. The ball should then be pushed away with the stick or kicked to the sidelines, not back into the danger area in the middle of the circle.

# Defence

The defence's main task is to prevent a goal being scored against their team, but they are also expected to gain possession, to set up attacks.

*One-on-one marking. Between the opponent and the goal, stay close, eyes on the ball.*

## DEFENSIVE AWARENESS

Defenders must mark attackers to prevent passes between them, to intercept passes or to force an error. The three main methods of marking are one-on-one, zonal marking or a combination of the two. In one-on-one, the marker should be positioned between the opponent and the goal, eyes on the ball. Zonal marking is where each defender takes charge of a particular area and any opponents who come into that area. In combination marking, it is one-on-one around the ball with the covering defenders in zones.

## DEFENDING SET PIECES

Only four players plus the goalkeeper are allowed to defend at penalty corners. The keeper is equipped to deal with shots on goal. One player advances from the line to obstruct the striker. Another is behind and left of the first defender, to cover passes to other attackers. The two other defenders cover the goal either side of the keeper.

*Defending a penalty corner. The goalkeeper organises the defence. It is important for defenders to practise the drill used at set pieces, such as penalties and free hits.*

16

*A reverse stick block, expertly performed*

## TECH TIPS – GRIP

*In the open grip, the left hand is at the top of the stick, with the right hand half way down. In the reverse position, the stick is turned by the left hand, and supported loosely by the right.*

*Open stick grip*

*Reverse stick grip*

## A UNITED FRONT

The defence is a team within a team. Wherever possible, the defence should work on tactics and strategy together in training sessions. Use attack versus defence drills, where the attackers outnumber the defenders.

## BLOCK AND TACKLE

Tackles should ideally see the defender gaining possession and setting up his or her team's attack. It is important to watch the ball and time the intervention correctly. Jockey for position and try to force your opponent on to the reverse stick side (the defender's open stick side).

*Helen Obialor of Nigeria defends against Malaysia's Rahman Nadia at the 2006 Commonwealth Games.*

## TECH TIPS – TACKLING

*Tackling opponents is a matter of timing and concentration. Stay balanced, don't dive in too soon, wait for the chance to strike.*

1 Open stick block – attacker is guided to defender's right, weight moves to left leg with stick held close to ground, forming barrier.

2 Reverse stick block – defender uses reverse stick if attacker moves to defender's left.

3 Jab tackle – head of stick is pushed towards ball, right leg providing force. Ball is struck at its base to move it up and away.

1

2

3

# Midfield

Being in the engine room of the team requires skill and stamina.

**TECH TIPS – PASSING**

*The most common methods of passing are shown here. But during a match, these tactics may not be possible – perhaps because your opponents can predict how you intend to pass if you stick to convention.*

## PLAYING THROUGH THE MIDDLE

No team can score a goal without having possession of the ball. The centre midfield is the route through which the defence can channel an attack. The midfielder also has a defensive role – winning the ball from the opposition.

*Once the ball is under control, be aware of the options. Which team mate is in the best position to receive a pass?*

## RECEIVING THE BALL

Players who can take a pass and instantly control it are invaluable. The open or reverse stick methods can be used for receiving a pass, before the player dribbles or shoots. Players should practise stopping the ball, before moving it on, as well as controlling the pass on the move.

*A player with good control wins extra space and time.*

## SKILL DRILL – PASSING

*Practise your passing and receiving skills with a team mate. Run parallel to each other, passing the ball between yourselves. Control the pass, dribble a few yards and pass it back. This is a simple, but invaluable skill.*

*Path taken by ball*

*Left player uses reverse stick to receive and pass ball.*

*Aim pass in front of receiver, so they can run on to it without stopping or slowing down.*

*Right player uses open stick to receive and pass ball.*

**1 THE PUSH** – *Hands apart, the body stays low, weight transfers from the right to left foot. As the right arm pushes forward, the left hand pulls back, giving power to the stroke.*

**2 THE REVERSE PUSH** – *For left-to-right passes, the stick is reversed and the ball struck using a short downswing.*

**3 THE SCOOP** – *Hands apart, the right foot is placed to the side of the ball, the left leg pushes weight forward and the stick head gets under the ball which is lifted into the air.*

**4 RECEIVING** – *Stay upright and balanced, keep your eyes and stick in line with the ball, keep the stick still and cushion the ball on impact.*

## PASSING THE BALL

Knowing when to pass and when to hold the ball can only be learned through practice. Three types of pass are shown above. Others are the 'hit', used for passing the ball quickly over longer distances; the 'slap' is similar to the push but harder over a long distance; the 'flick' is used to lift the ball into the air. For passing to be effective in match situations, the passer must know which team mate is in the best position to receive a pass, and be in control of the ball.

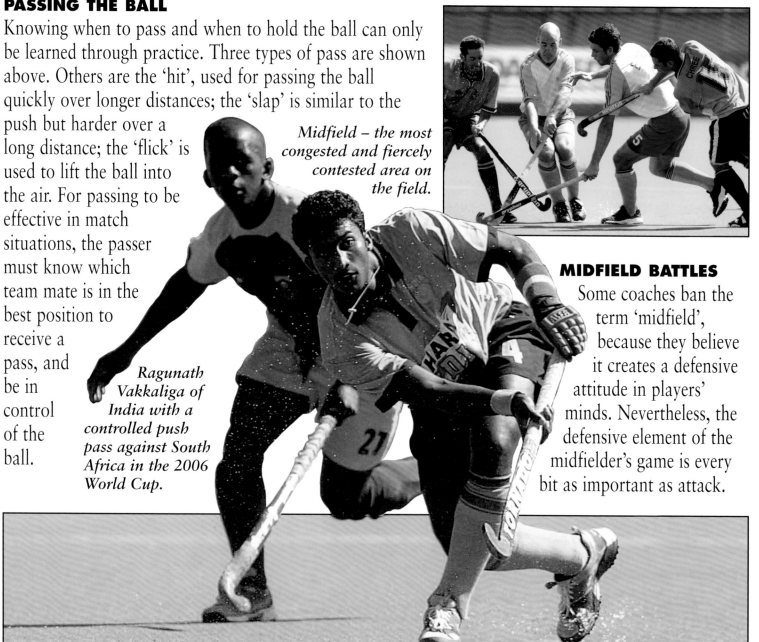

*Midfield – the most congested and fiercely contested area on the field.*

*Ragunath Vakkaliga of India with a controlled push pass against South Africa in the 2006 World Cup.*

### MIDFIELD BATTLES

Some coaches ban the term 'midfield', because they believe it creates a defensive attitude in players' minds. Nevertheless, the defensive element of the midfielder's game is every bit as important as attack.

*If you keep the ball under close control, your opponent has less chance of making a successful tackle.*

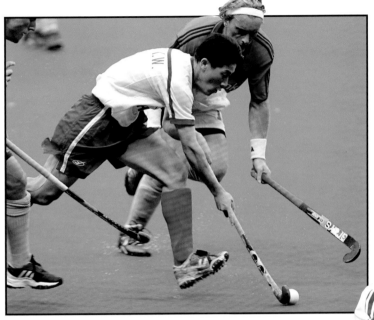

# Attack

**A**ttacking play in hockey means much more than simply blasting shots towards the goal.

### CLOSE CONTROL

Keeping possession of the ball is essential. Surrendering the ball too easily to the opposition results in the loss of the game. If you practise keeping possession of the ball, you will soon build up the confidence to keep defenders at bay.

### DRIBBLING

While hockey is essentially a passing game, there will be times when a pass is not possible. For example, if the opposition successfully marks you, dribbling the ball or running with it under control of the stick might be necessary. Once a player has learned how to dribble, he or she should practise dummying or dodging to outwit any opponents.

### TECH TIPS – DRIBBLING

*When dribbling at speed, it is important to keep the ball in a position where the legs move at a natural stride, not too close or too far ahead.*

*Basic open stick dribble – The ball is ahead and to the right of the feet. The head is held up, making passes easier to spot.*

*Indian dribble – 1 The ball is moved forwards from right to left. 2 The stick is reversed ... 3 ... and the ball is moved from left to right.*

1

2

3

*Having beaten the opponent, look for the passing options.*

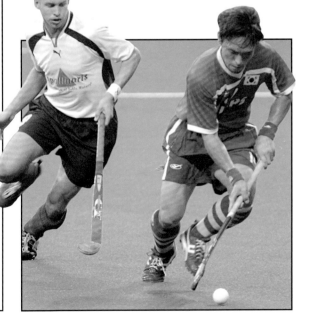

*Keeping your eyes on the ball is the key to success in any ball game.*

## TECH TIPS – DODGING

*Dodging means outwitting and beating an opponent in a one-on-one situation. It is important that the ball is under tight control – if it is too far ahead, the opponent can easily make the tackle. No defender can make contact with an attacker's body or stick when making a tackle, so the advantage is with the dribbler.*

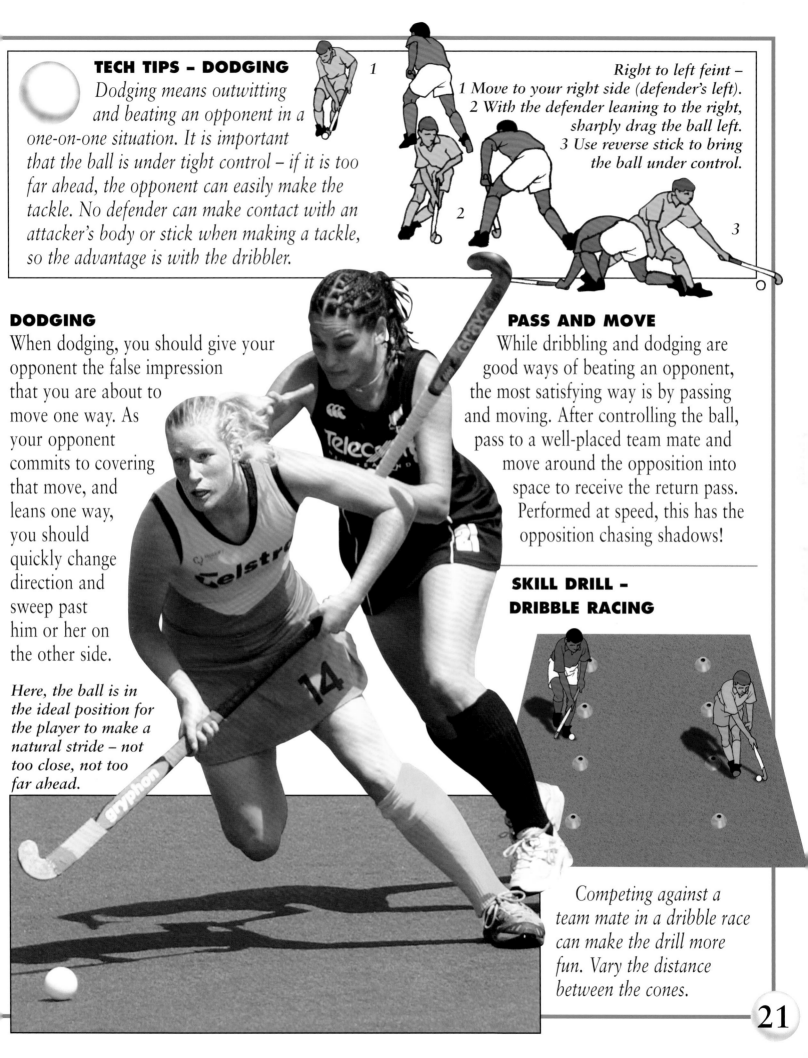

*Right to left feint –*
*1 Move to your right side (defender's left).*
*2 With the defender leaning to the right, sharply drag the ball left.*
*3 Use reverse stick to bring the ball under control.*

## DODGING

When dodging, you should give your opponent the false impression that you are about to move one way. As your opponent commits to covering that move, and leans one way, you should quickly change direction and sweep past him or her on the other side.

*Here, the ball is in the ideal position for the player to make a natural stride – not too close, not too far ahead.*

## PASS AND MOVE

While dribbling and dodging are good ways of beating an opponent, the most satisfying way is by passing and moving. After controlling the ball, pass to a well-placed team mate and move around the opposition into space to receive the return pass. Performed at speed, this has the opposition chasing shadows!

## SKILL DRILL – DRIBBLE RACING

*Competing against a team mate in a dribble race can make the drill more fun. Vary the distance between the cones.*

21

# Teamwork

No player, no matter how skilful, can win a match alone. Communication within the team is essential.

*Team talks harness team spirit. Encouragement is essential, and being aware of the game plan is vital.*

## ATTACKING AS A TEAM

To create openings in the opposition's defence, your team needs to be able to change the point of attack, to pass the ball out to the wings to stretch the defence, and pull players out of position by constant movement off the ball. Consequently, every player in the attacking team has a part to play.

*Attack as a team, supporting your team mates all the way.*

## DEFENDING AS A TEAM

When the opposition has the ball, the defenders must adopt their positions quickly, otherwise the attack will reach the goal. They must defend as soon as possession is lost. In the opposition's circle, forwards should try to delay the ball being cleared, to allow their own defenders to take up position.

*Defenders*

*Defensive triangle*

*Attack*

*Attack aims to disrupt defensive shape and create space.*

*Defence aims to maintain shape and cover attackers.*

## SKILL DRILL – ATTACK AND DEFENCE

*This is a useful exercise at training sessions. Match your team's attack and defence against each other. Concentrate on special parts of the game, such as attacking down the flanks, so that the defence can become accustomed to using the sideline as a barrier for the opposition.*

*Defending a penalty corner – do the job you've been assigned.*

## SET PIECES

Set pieces occur when the referee blows for an infringement or when the ball goes out of play. The eight set pieces are penalty corners, penalty strokes, corners, free hits, 16-yard hits, hit- or push-ins, the push back and the bully. The attack and defence should both practise moves to master their set pieces.

**TECH TIPS – PENALTY OR SHORT CORNERS** *Defending sides can only use four players plus the goalkeeper within the circle. The rest must be beyond the half-way line. Attacking players may be anywhere on the field except in the circle, except of course the player putting the ball into play.*

*Defenders have to be ready to combat the attacking side's tricks.*

*Attackers attempt to deceive the defence with decoy runners and strikers.*

*Taeke Taekema of the Netherlands – prolific scorer from penalty corners with a push flick for goal.*

**TECH TIPS – FORMATIONS** *Your team should make use of the special abilities available from each player. This may mean altering formation to accommodate a sweeper or an extra midfielder.*

*1-2-3-5 – the basic attacking formation*

*1-1-3-2-4 – sweeper strengthens defence.*

*1-1-3-3-3 – midfield gives team flexibility.*

23

# Going for goal

**I**t's a simple idea – the team that scores the largest number of goals wins. But putting the ball into the net is more difficult than it seems.

### HITTING THE TARGET

Most goals in hockey, apart from direct shots after penalty corners, are scored from within a 10-metre radius of the goal. Even from that distance, accuracy cannot be guaranteed. You can improve your chances by staying balanced. The first shot of a penalty corner must remain under 460 mm high unless it is flicked.

### STRENGTH AND SPEED

Obviously, the harder a player can hit a shot and the quicker the ball travels towards the goal, the more chance it has of eluding the goalkeeper and finding the back of the net. But hard shots are not just a matter of how strong a player is – timing is a key factor, and taking your eyes off the ball could easily result in a scuffed shot.

*Even a goalkeeper wearing full kit can't protect every part of the goal.*

*The slap hit is a low-body position, with the right hand down the stick with, as ever, eyes on the ball.*

### SKILL DRILL – ACCURATE SHOOTING

*This drill helps shooting and balance. On a signal, the keeper runs to the five-yard mark and back. At the same time, the striker dribbles the ball around a cone placed five yards from the top of the D, returns and shoots at goal.*

*Repeat drill with cone to left of goal.*

*Adjust cone distance, so that shot coincides with keeper getting back in position.*

## TECH TIPS – SHOOTING

*A good goal-scorer never has to think about which shot to use – it is just a natural reaction. But you can only develop this level of instinct by practising hard. Try to add as many shooting techniques to your repertoire as you can.*

**1 THE HIT** – *Hands together at the top of the stick, the left foot moves alongside the ball. Your weight shifts to the left leg, as your arms swing down. Straighten your wrists as the ball is struck. The stick follows the direction of the ball.*

**2 THE SLAP** – *Similar to the hit shot, but the right hand is further down the stick and the body is lower. The right arm gives the ball speed.*
**3 THE FLICK** – *With hands apart, the weight shifts to the left leg as the stick head lifts the ball. Hold the ball for as long as possible before flicking it away.*

## POISE AND BALANCE

As soon as the ball has been controlled in the circle, the attacker should shoot as quickly as possible, to prevent the goalkeeper moving into a covering position. Ideally, the striker should be well balanced with a good body position.

*Following through helps direct the shot on target.*

*It is not always possible to remain balanced at speed.*

## STAYING SHARP

Regular goal-scorers should be prepared to shoot at any time. The successful striker should leave the opposition off-balance. Your chances of shooting and scoring, whether by speed or by stealth, can be increased with practice. Strikers who regularly find the net always boost the morale of their team.

# Hockey variations

Stick and ball games are common throughout the world. New styles are always being added to this range of sports.

## HURLING

Like hockey, hurling is renowned as one of the fastest team games in the world. It is a national sport in Ireland, administered by the Gaelic Athletic Association. A 15-a-side game, the object is to drive the 4.5 oz (127 g) ball through goalposts 21 feet high and 21 feet apart. As in rugby, there is a crossbar, eight feet from the ground. Three points are scored when the ball goes under the bar, one point when it goes over. In Scotland, shinty is closely related to hurling and hockey.

## LACROSSE

Lacrosse is a ten-a-side game. You score by throwing the 5 oz (142 g) rubber ball into a six foot square goal. The lacrosse racquet, or crosse, is shaped like a hockey stick with a triangular net at the end for catching and holding the ball.

*Unlike in hockey, personal contact, such as shoulder charging, is allowed in lacrosse.*

*The matches between Kilkenny and Tipperary, in the All Ireland Hurling tournament, are always a sell-out at Croke Park in Dublin.*

*Ice hockey is the most popular team sport in Canada. Here the Montreal Canadiens take on the Ottawa Senators in Quebec.*

# MINI HOCKEY

Mini hockey was developed to provide an introduction to the game, and a basic grounding for young players. Learning the skills of hockey with a small stick and smaller, lighter balls has encouraged many eight- to ten-year-olds to progress to the full game when they are older.

No centre line

Just one umpire

Octopush – not for the faint-hearted. Only decent swimmers need apply.

## ICE HOCKEY

Ice hockey in its modern form dates back to the 1860s, when the game was played on the frozen Kingston Harbour in Ontario. Canada remains a stronghold of the game, with teams playing in the National Hockey League (NHL) in the USA – the foremost professional league in the world. In the UK, there have been various attempts to popularize the sport since the 1920s. Currently ten teams play in the Elite League from all over the country, including Belfast, Cardiff and Edinburgh.

## ODD HOCKEY

Ever heard of octopush? This strange development of the game is played underwater! Another adaptation, taking in elements of both hockey and ice hockey, is roller hockey. Hockey on rollerskates became an international sport in 1910, when an inter-club tournament was held in Paris. The first European Championships were staged in England in 1926.

# The world of hockey

Hockey's international status was officially recognised in 1924 with the founding in Paris of the Fédération Internationale de Hockey.

### HOCKEY TODAY

The game is now played in almost 100 countries on six continents. It is a major sport in India and Pakistan, widely played throughout Europe and also in South Africa and Australia. In South America, Argentina is now a major force, especially in the women's game.

*In India, children are encouraged to play hockey from an early age.*

### THE WORLD CUP

Hockey grew enormously in popularity between 1970 and 1980. The European Cup was inaugurated in 1970. A year later, the first World Cup was held and won, not surprisingly, by Pakistan who have taken the men's world title on four occasions. The Women's World Cup was established in 1974 and has been dominated by the Netherlands, winners in Madrid in 2006 for the sixth time. The 2010 edition will be staged in Argentina.

*The top hockey nations compete for the World Cup. There have been ten men's tournaments so far. After Pakistan, the most successful men's teams have come from the Netherlands, who have won three times.*

### WORLD CUP WINNERS

*Germany and the Netherlands will be the defending champions in 2010.*

| MEN | WOMEN |
| --- | --- |
| 1 Pakistan (1971, 1978, 1982, 1994) | 1 Netherlands (1974, 1978, 1983, 1986, 1990, 2006) |
| 2 Netherlands (1973, 1990, 1998) | 2 West Germany (1976, 1981) |
| 3 Germany (2002, 2006) | 3 Australia (1994, 1998) |
| 4 Australia (1986) | 4 Argentina (2002) |
| 5 India (1975) | |

*Spain have twice won silver at the Olympics, but in 2004 were pipped for bronze by Germany.*

## THE OLYMPICS

Men's hockey was included in the Olympics for the first time in London, in 1908. Four of the six teams involved were from Britain, and the England team took the gold. India dominated the Olympics from 1928 to 1956, winning all six gold medals without losing a single game. In 2004, Europe's domination of the men's event was broken by Australia in Athens, when they beat the Netherlands 2-1 in the final. The Netherlands also lost in the women's event in 2004 – beaten 2-1 by Germany in the final.

*Team GB won gold in the 2007 Australian Youth Olympic Festival, beating the hosts 4-2 in the final.*

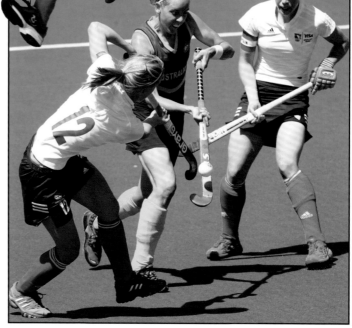

## CHAMPIONS' TROPHY

The demand for more international tournaments led to the establishment of the Champions' Trophy in 1978, now held each year for the six top-ranked teams. The nine times mens' winners, Germany, beat Australia 1-0 in the 2007 final in Malaysia, while in the women's competition in Argentina, the Netherlands beat the host nation 1-0.

29

# Staying fit

Fitness is essential if you're to last the pace for 70 minutes.

To enjoy the game to the full, you need to stay fit. Training helps you to prepare for matches, prevents injuries and speeds up recovery.

## HEALTHY EATING

Players who do not stick to a healthy, balanced diet are soon found out at top level. Eat foods from the basic groups – dairy products, meat, fish and chicken, fruit, vegetables and cereals – and you should absorb enough vitamins and energy. On training or match days, eat a couple of hours before the start, then drink liquids – plain water is best – to prevent dehydration.

## EXERCISE

Use the pre-season period to build up stamina and strength. A full game lasts 70 minutes, during which you will be expected to sprint, run and turn without tiring. Mix sprint drills with longer distance running, time your runs and aim to improve each time. Gym work can improve your strength. During the season, work on flexibility. As well as team training to improve understanding and skills, try the circuit drill carrying a hockey stick. Running, jumping and turning with the stick will become second nature – a useful asset on the field. And don't forget to warm up before each match.

## TECH TIPS – KEEPING THE TANK FULL

*On match days, eat breakfast about six hours before the start, with foods that are easily digestible. Sip liquids through the morning. Lunch should also be easily digestible. Beware of drinking too many heavy liquids during the match. In the evening, replace all that lost energy!*

*Timetable for match day. Try to stick to the same routine each time. You might feel like eating a huge lunch, but you'll feel better if you don't!*

**12pm,** Light lunch – Pasta or jacket potato with beans or cottage cheese

Liquids

**8am, Breakfast –** fruit juice, cereal or porridge, fruit, yoghurt, toast with jam or honey

**3pm, The match –** liquids during game, banana at half-time

**7pm, Dinner –** meal rich in carbohydrates and proteins, isotonic drink

Liquids

Liquids

*(clock face showing 12, 1, 2, 3, 4, 5, 6, 7, 8, 9, 10, 11)*

## SKILL DRILL – FEELING THE BURN

*Circuit training in the gym is an ideal way to keep fit. Set up four or five different exercise areas. One might be for bench steps, another for press-ups, a third for skipping. Rest for 45 seconds after each circuit.*

20 m

1 Dribble around cones.
2 Jog. 3 Do ten sit-ups.
4 Sprint. 5 Jog.
6 Do ten press-ups.

# Glossary

DEHYDRATION loss of fluids in the body, resulting in energy loss

DRIBBLING running with the ball under close control

DUMMYING making to go one way, then confusing the opponent by darting the other

FEINT first move when dummying

MARK being close enough to an opponent to tackle or intercept a pass

OFFSIDE an attacker is offside inside the 25-yard line if there are fewer than two defenders between him and the goal

ONE-ON-ONE when one defender marks one attacker

OPEN STICK normal stick position with the toe outwards

PROSTHETIC artificial, usually plastic, referring to protective kit

REVERSE STICK stick position with the toe inwards

SET PIECE methods of restarting the game, such as penalty corners and free hits, after the ball has gone out of play or infringements

SYNTHETIC artificial, referring to playing surfaces other than natural grass

ZONAL MARKING when players mark areas, not opponents

# Further information

*Sport England*
*3rd Floor, Victoria House,*
*Bloomsbury Square,*
*London,*
*WC1B 4SE*
*http://www.sportengland.org*

*England Hockey*
*The National Hockey Stadium,*
*Silbury Boulevard,*
*Milton Keynes,*
*MK9 1HA*
*http://www.englandhockey.co.uk*

*Great Britain Hockey Ltd*
*Bisham Abbey NSC,*
*Nr Marlow,*
*Buckinghamshire,*
*SL7 1RT*
*http://www.greatbritainhockey.co.uk*

*International Hockey Federation*
*Residence du Parc,*
*Rue du Valentin 61,*
*1004 Lausanne,*
*Switzerland,*
*http://www.worldhockey.org or www.fihockey.org*

*Hockey Australia*
*Level 1,*
*433-435 South Road,*
*Bentleigh,*
*VIC 3204*
*http://www.hockey.org.au*

*International Olympic Committee*
*Château de Vidy,*
*1007 Lausanne,*
*Switzerland*
*http://www.olympic.org/uk*

# Index